Blockchain

Understand Blockchain in a Day: A Comprehensive Introduction to the Basics of Blockchain & Cryptocurrencies

Steve Gold

Table of contents

Introduction

If you have an interest in Bitcoin, there is a good chance that you have heard about the technology underlying it that guarantees it remains secure — Blockchain. What you may not have been aware of, however, is that Blockchain can be used in a range of different applications. If you are not familiar with Bitcoin or Blockchain, it is time to sit up and take notice - In a world where it is becoming increasingly important to secure our data online, it is clear that Blockchain will become more and more important going forward.

In this book, we will cover the basics of what Blockchain is and how it works, as well as taking a look at some of the history behind it, what you need to take note of, the likely future of Blockchain, how re‑ lates to Bitcoin and how it is changing the way our fi‑ nancial services industry works.

Blockchain is an innovative system that packs a real punch when it comes to protecting data online, and it is definitely worth knowing about.

Chapter One

What is Blockchain?

The beauty of Blockchain when it comes to protecting our data is that there is no single creator. Entries are added and checked by different contributors and so a "block" of transactions are created. The security of this system is due to the fact that multiple verifica tions are carried out. Also, as the data is stored in blocks from different sources, rather than as a single entity, the system's security is increased further. – ac tually, it is virtually impossible to hack or amend the data in the system because there are so many people inputting and checking it.

Building a house is a good analogy for how the system works – first, the foundation is laid and checked for sturdiness. When this has been deemed satisfactory, bricks are added one at a time to make up the walls of the house. A building inspector will check that the building is being carried out properly and give clearance for the project to continue. If one of the builders decides to make changes, they have to do so with the permission of any others involved in the project. No one person will build the entire house – you will need to call in roofers and plumbers, etc. and each will do their bit – and so you have a lot more eyes on the project.

By the same token, Blockchain uses different makers and checkers. Each individual is given part of the information to input or check. No one person in this process has access to all the data and, most of the time, they will not even be aware of what it is that they are inputting as a whole. As a result, they never receive the full details necessary to enable them to misuse the information for crimes such as identity theft. In addition, the maker and checkers' IP addresses are recorded making all data input traceable.

Each person does their bit and inputs their bits of data, thus building up the whole. The transactions are linked via a timestamp to the block preceding them. In addition, the data is spread over a number of different computers so that even if one has been compromised, the data is safe.

These blockchains are essentially an online ledger that has been distributed piecemeal.

The system can be held in the public domain, as is the case with Bitcoin, or kept private within a private network as required. Individual makers are able to add information reasonably easily but changing or deleting information is a lot harder.

In order to change blocks previously set out, your proposed changes will be submitted to the other computers within the network. They will run security algorithms to ascertain whether or not these changes are valid in terms of past behavior within the chain.

The network will make the decision whether or not the changes are legit based on whether or not they are within the norm for that chain and who the person making the changes is. This adds a very real layer of security that is a lot tougher to crack.

So, what stops a hacker just adding information that they like? The network also verifies new data being added to the chain, in order to confirm that it comes from a legitimate source.

The following is verified by the network for new additions and changes and adds to the security of the network as a whole:

Consensus

Most of the members of the chain need to agree that the event being recorded did actually happen.

Consistency

The new information or change needs to be a valid continuation of the previous block or, at the very least, information that would logically fit with the previous block.

Transaction

The network checks that the information is unique and is not contradicted by other data input in the same chain.

Automated Conflict Identifiers

The system monitors itself to identify possible conflicts within the structure.

This can assist companies with cost reduction when it comes to layers of security within the organization.

Say, for example, that your company needs to process twenty transactions at a time.

Previously each transaction would need to its own digital fingerprint as verification when it was passed over to the relevant service provider. This can be time-con suming but is important in order to prevent fraud.

If we instead use a blockchain, we can combine all twenty transactions under a single digital fingerprint. All participants within the chain are able to see the digital fingerprint and this will tell them that the group of transactions is valid.

Each company will have its own digital fingerprint, allowing the company to keep track of all transactions linked to that fingerprint.

Chapter Two

The History Behind Blockchain

The story of Blockchain and how it was developed is a fairly interesting one. Satoshi Nakamoto first coined the term and gave a definition of what it meant in 2008 before blockchain itself became a reality.

The concept became a reality in 2009 when it was first incorporated into the code for Bitcoin. This initial design became a trendsetter in the field and was soon adopted by other cryptocurrencies as well. In the next five years, its use had been extended to more than eighty different applications.

It was in 2014 when blockchain 2.0 was initially released with a focus being more on the differentiation of blockchain and Bitcoin and their different roles – Bitcoin is an asset that is to be secured and kept track of; blockchain is the infrastructural system that makes this possible.

The system was developed further to enable the use of scalable features and to add in even more functionality. In the first half of 2014, there were a minimum of eight separate projects that were being developed using the blockchain idea as a means of distribution.

Fast-forward to 2016 and blockchain has grown from strength to strength, being recognized as one of the ways forward when it comes to securing sensitive data. The Russian Federation has adopted blockchain 2.0 as a means of securing its security depository.

The system has also been embraced by parts of the music industry's regulatory structures in order to develop a system that can be used to accurately keep track of royalties to be paid and to keep help manage copyright issues globally.

At this present point in time, blockchain is acknowledged as an industry disruptor because of its unique method of securing data. That said, it is still in its in fancy and we have not yet seen the full scope of what it can do.

Chapter 3

Why you Should Take Note of Blockchain

So, you basically understand a little more about blockchain now. In this chapter, we will go through what it is that you need to know about it and its future.

Blockchain is most often brought up in relation to Bitcoin but it is not Bitcoin-specific. It is rather the structure that underlies the Bitcoin system and can be ap

plied to a range of different applications as well.

For now, most alternative applications are using Blockchain as a basis for financial transactions or data storage but this really is only the tip of the iceberg.

Blockchain is ideal for creating databases for any information that you like. Take the project Storj, for example. It allows us to set up a profile and access cloud-based storage secured by Blockchain.

What is Great About Blockchain?

No one can say for certain where it will end up. We have only an inkling of how useful this technology can be at the moment.

Twenty years ago, people would undoubtedly have scoffed at the idea that spreading out a database over a range of nodes stored on different computers would make the information more secure.

Today we are acknowledging that, despite the extensive security measures put in place to guard server farms, their centralized location is what makes them the most vulnerable.

The system is open-source. Anyone is able to work on it and adjust the code to fit their needs. This is a large part of the reason why the possibilities with Blockchain are pretty much limitless.

Think how far we have come in terms of computer software. From the very earliest programs that required you to type in every command, to the completely autonomous systems we have now, we have been advancing at an extremely fast rate.

The system is secure. Very strong encryptions are utilized and these have not been cracked ever. The way it is designed also makes it possible to detect entries that have been altered or forged easily.

Also, with the number of different users involved in verifying the data, it becomes a lot more difficult for those trying to forge information within the system to succeed.

The data is not under the control of a particular institution or government. It runs completely independently. Information within the system is not subject to the whims of some or other large corporate or government official.

Server downtime is now a thing of the past. With the data being spread across numerous computers, the likelihood that every single computer in the network going down at the same time are minuscule.

So even if the vast majority of the computers went off-line, the network would be able to build itself up again.

Quite simply, blockchain is something that is completely unique. It is going to change the way we use and store data forever. It allows us to streamline processes and lets us do many things that simply we not possible before.

Chapter 4

The Future of Blockchain

A number of the world's largest and best-known financial institutions have been conducting experiments into how they can make use of Blockchain. It is widely acknowledged that it is no longer a case of if Blockchain is going to revolutionize the financial sector but more a case of when it will happen.

Blockchain has been growing from strength to strength in the last few years. It is expected to grow exponentially once it becomes more widely adopted.

Whilst it is not considered mainstream yet, it is certainly knocking on the door.

So basically, it's time to watch this space as far as blockchain is concerned.

As more and more of the larger organizations and corporations in the world are becoming interested, more money is being directed into the development of blockchain applications.

And that is what is so exciting – we may not know what we will be using blockchain for in the coming years but we do know that it is here to stay.

The Internet of Things

If you're not a techie, this is probably not a term that you are familiar with. Basically, all it means is that all physical objects are able to have their own online identities.

We've started seeing this already in Smart TV and Smart Car technology but it will roll out to other items as well. So, just like your laptop, everything capable of internet connectivity in your home will have its own identity – like an IP address.

So, what is this likely to mean for us? We will be able to remotely access these items. Already there are kettles that allow you to activate them remotely and fridges that can monitor food levels and put through an order when things run low.

But what about other applications? Like self-driven cars that are able to avoid accidents because they all have an online identity? It's kind of like cyber-stalking the person you are interested in. You make sure that you know where they are at all times so you know when to avoid them or when to accidentally run into them.

The cars on the road will start to be able to communicate with one another and, while there are problems that must be ironed out, this looks like it will be a positive development. It could conceivably reduce the road accident rate substantially.

But it goes further than that as well – intelligent cars are just the start. We can now look forward to a whole new interconnected world going forward.

And it's not that far off. It has started already and it is estimated that we could be looking at an integrative "Internet of Things" as early as 2020.

The Internet of Things and Blockchain

It seems simple, just assign every item its own online identity and the "Internet of Things" is a reality.

The problem is that it is logistically not as simple as that.

If we use the means traditionally available to us, the cost would be prohibitive. It would entail each retailer maintaining a large number of server farms and en suring that these are secure.

And these would have to be maintained throughout the lifetime of the products concerned.

Security is of paramount concern here. You don't want someone to be able to take control of your car, for example.

And of course, there is the issue of potential downtime as well. Imagine the chaos if a server went down and a whole range of self-driven cars were not able to function as a result.

Blockchain is being looked on as a solution to these issues.

Industry giants, Samsung and IBM have already alluded to the fact. Using a blockchain as a base for the data helps to reduce costs by spreading out the storage of that data over a number of different computers.

The system is secure and so security concerns are minimized. Changes must be authorized by others on the network instead of the current set of maker/checker that involves just one or two people.

In addition, the data being spread over a number of different computers means that potential downtime is almost completely eliminated.

More Transparency When It Comes to Supply Chains

Many people feel that companies have become untrustworthy as regards the sourcing of goods, etc. For those people, blockchain offers a viable solution.

You can now safely input tracking data showing the full journey of the goods from source to the company online.

This can easily be read and utilized by consumers who are concerned about how the goods were sourced.

Whilst companies are able to make their supply chains from source available as it is now, this is not always a reliable record.

The traditional chain relies on individual components entering the data. This makes it a lot easier to commit fraud.

With a blockchain, no one company in the list from source to end consumer will be able to alter the list. The information will be provided in a continuous chain.

This makes fraud a lot less likely to occur.

Online Security

Handing your personal information over to anyone is always a risk. Large companies that have centralized data storage servers are a tempting target for hackers.

And there have been a lot of cases where such companies have been hacked, leaving their client's information exposed.

Blockchain can provide a solution here as well. Without one single centralized source of data, the entire database is less prone to being hacked.

In addition, the data can easily be verified within the system and cannot be altered without the approval of numerous users.

Blockchain has made it possible for companies to create apps that allow users to create their own central profiles. Their personal data is stored on the blockchain and you then use the centralized ID when using other sites.

So basically, you only really have to remember one name and password. You then use this when accessing sites.

The next step would be to create a digital financial profile. Something similar to PayPal, for example.

Where you set up a central profile, link your cards and then buy online using the profile rather than giving out personal credit card details.

The truth is that we really have no idea how far this is going to take us in future. In a world where information can be safely shared and is always available, the possibilities are endless.

Chapter 5

Blockchain as a Part of the Bitcoin Family

Blockchain can operate without Bitcoin but the two are indelibly linked. And this is not necessarily a good thing. Whilst Bitcoin has been repairing its reputation, memories of the Silk Road scandal still remain.

The Silk Road, in case you were unaware, was an online marketplace where denizens of the dark web sold illegal items. These items were anything from drugs to child pornography and even sex slaves.

Bitcoin itself didn't actually have a hand in these transactions or promoting them but it was the currency used by those listing the items.

Thus, when the FBI shut the marketplace down, Bitcoin lost a lot in terms of value and reputation.

Does Bitcoin Promote Criminality?

Those who come out against Bitcoin often tout the above example as a means to explain why Bitcoin should be scrapped. This is somewhat unfair, though.

The idea behind the cryptocurrency is a good one and the truth is that, with any system, criminals will look for a way to exploit it.

Is the answer scrapping the currency completely? Is the answer discarding the underlying infrastructure because it could be used by criminals?

Clearly, the answer is that this is not the way to go.

Bitcoin Does Have Market Value

Bitcoins have been traded on the market for some years now and have seen a consequent increase in value. The value does change depending on demand, just like other traded commodities.

And, also like other traded commodities, there is a finite number of Bitcoins – the total number of Bitcoins that can be issued is 21 000 000. When that figure is reached, no more will be issued.

It is interesting to note that at the time of publishing this book, there are currently in the range of

15 200 000 Bitcoins in circulation so we are nearing that final number.

Bitcoin is the first payment system to use Blockchain as its infrastructure. As an experiment for potential future cryptocurrencies, it would seem that it has been a success.

It will certainly be interesting to see what happens when Bitcoins have finally run their course. Will they become more valuable or will interest flag?

If nothing else, this has been a valuable test of the Blockchain concept. A lot of lessons have been learned with the running of Bitcoin.

One thing is certain, Blockchain and Bitcoin are both innovative and complete industry disruptors.

That they have changed the face of the internet is true and that Blockchain will continue to shape the internet is also true. Whatever else is said about them, this cannot be denied.

Chapter Six

Blockchain is Changing the Face of the Financial Industry

For over three decades, people have been trying to use cryptography to help to secure financial transactions online. The problem is that because of the number of intermediaries involved, leaks were inevitable.

Credit card transactions, in particular, were very risky because of the amount of data that needed to be disclosed and prohibitively expensive when it came to smaller transactions.

What it essentially boils down to when buying online is how much you can trust the person that you are divulging your credit card details to.

Satoshi Nakamoto's idea for blockchain and the use of cryptocurrencies does away with the need for a third party, making it possible to establish "trust" immediately through coding.

Essentially the transactions are made directly peer to peer and authenticated through a system of mass collaboration as opposed to the traditional system where a third party, motivated by profit, facilitates the trans action. You won't even need a bank account or credit card.

The source code is open-based, meaning that you can download it for nothing and it can be used to develop a range of applications that allow for the management of online transactions.

The potential range of applications that might be developed is staggering and it can truly be said that blockchain will transform a number of different online applications in future.

Blockchains are being adopted in the financial sector by some of the biggest players and even by the governments of some countries – as a way to improve the speed of transactions, improve the security of transactions and databases and to reduce costs to the end consumer.

Not all of these applications involve the use of a cryptocurrency when it comes to payments, though.

It is, however, the blockchains that have been developed on the original Bitcoin model that look set to have the largest impact on the traditional finance industry.

Blockchains based on this model are not stored in one file on one server – they are recorded in a global ledger and the approval of every transaction is not up to one single resource – the files are spread over the network onto various computers, making it impossible to hack because there is simply no longer a single data source.

The blockchain is visible to anyone within the network and so there is no need to have a specific organization keeping the records or verifying transactions.

The blockchain itself is also heavily encrypted to further protect the data – it cannot be changed without the approval of others within the change.

It is kind of like when you go access your safe deposit box – you and the bank official each has a key so that neither can open the safe deposit box without the other.

There is no need to worry about your personal details being on a system that hasn't employed the strongest encryption or worrying about a corrupt staff member selling or misusing your information.

With blockchain, a check is done each 10 minutes to verify, clear and store any transactions that have been entered. Each block added has to be linked to the block before it in order to be valid.

Essentially this gives each link in the chain a time-stamp and digital trail that cannot be destroyed – you would literally have to rewrite everything in the chain from the beginning. This is virtually impossible to do.

What you end up with is a ledger that is distributed over a vast network of computers, with each and every transaction verified and recorded from the beginning.

Transactions are subjected to far more checks before being approved and any changes are recorded permanently.

And for data management, anything that has value can be recorded – from ownership of property to where your food comes from – anything that can be represented in code can be recorded.

It is quite a mind-boggling concept – there is very little that cannot be recorded and reconciled in real time. This is a whole new way of sharing data that is important to us. In fact, it will completely revolution

ize the way we view and share data going forward.

Chapter 7

Possible Issues Going Forward

So, if Blockchain is so fantastic, why has everything not been changed yet? There are still some issues that need to be ironed out.

We Are Not Ready with the Infrastructure Yet

There might be those that disagree with this statement but the truth is that not enough people have a good understanding of how Blockchain works.

Whilst this is changing, the infrastructure that is needed to implement the system on a global scale is simply not in place.

If you were in the DRC, for example, would you be able to go into a bank and buy Bitcoins? It is not likely because the infrastructure is simply not at that level yet.

Secondly, to suddenly add millions of people would literally overtax the current system. It is simply not ready for that kind of increase in traffic.

The current system does not have the capacity to carry the amount of information that this would entail.

Then you would have to deal with the vast number of people who have little to no understanding of how this actually works.

Their lack of understanding could mean that they end up becoming very frustrated with blockchain and decide that it is not something that they wish to adopt as a whole.

Blockchain technology at this moment in time is not all that user-friendly with some specialized knowledge required in order to be able to use it effectively.

Take a look at a Bitcoin wallet address, for example. This could be as long as 36 characters and is usually just a string of numbers and letters.

We are used to going to a search engine and typing in our keywords. This would never work when it came to a Bitcoin wallet and is something that developers of new Blockchain apps would need to consider as well.

Things Take Too Long to Verify

In the grand scheme of things, financial transactions conducted via Blockchain can be verified pretty quickly. In fact, this is one of the advantages for financial institutions looking into implementing the system.

Having said that, it still takes around 10 minutes to verify a transaction. Now, whilst that may not always be such a big deal with some financial transactions, it could have very negative effects with time sensitive ones.

Let's say, for example, you were purchasing stock. Would you want to have to wait ten minutes for the purchase to go through? You could end up losing a lot of money because of the time lag.

Other real-world applications of Blockchain might also be negatively affected by this. Let's say, for example, your Smart car is driving on the road and it needs to interact with another car to avoid a collision.

In a situation where split-seconds make a difference, ten minutes might seem like an eternity.

Records Would Last Forever

You likely wouldn't think that would be much of a problem, would you? But what if you had defaulted on your car payment or had your car repossessed?

Under the current system, the black mark would be recorded against your name but would fall away after the debt has been paid or after a set number of years.

With Blockchain, this would become impossible – the record cannot be changed without rewriting the whole stream.

And whilst you may have made the mistake some time ago, everyone who views your financial record will be able to see that it was made.

And credit checks have become compulsory not only for new credit applications but also for many job applications as well.

It is Going to Take a Lot of Energy to Sustain

According to an article by Nathan Schneider, the management of the Bitcoin system in 2015 resulted in

$100 million of costs in terms of energy used. Now that was to secure only $3 billion dollars.

Now imagine if the largest financial institutions or governments and millions of people globally started making use of the Blockchain software.

Running the checks to ensure the safety of the system on billions of entries will use a staggering amount of electricity.

There are those that believe that this one aspect will be the largest obstacle when it comes to large-scale implementation of Blockchain. The carbon footprint will be enormous.

Having said that, we do have to factor in that the current system of storing information in server farms does also use a lot of energy.

Server farms need to be kept cool to prevent overheating and loss of data. The energy requirements are thus also large.

If Blockchain software is adopted, the reliance on server farms would be reduced.

Of course, with technology progressing at the rate at which it does, faster processing speeds may help to reduce this negative impact.

It's New Territory Legally

Blockchain has a lot of potential but our current legal systems may need to be adapted to deal with it. And that means that more regulation is on the cards if blockchain systems become widely accepted.

The problem is that those in charge of regulating the systems may not fully understand them. And if they do not understand them properly, how can they prop erly regulate them?

Lawmakers will have to guard against those who use the software for illegal purposes. We have already seen, in Bitcoin, that the systems provide an ideal platform to pay for illegal transactions such as terrorism, human trafficking, etc. And it is obvious that they need to guard against such things. This level of regulation could annoy users.

What could happen is that someone develops a system that is better in terms of privacy, etc. and Blockchain becomes old news again.

And what happens when people work within the system to fund a crime? Let's say, for example, a child is kidnapped and killed. What if the parents are not satisfied with the punishment of the killer? They could ostensibly fund a transaction that will be paid out to someone who kills that person.

In order for the money to be paid out, the transaction will need to be vetted by numerous people. Essentially that means that, whilst the parents are responsible for instigating the murder of the child killer, there could be thousands of people who may be considered complicit because they authorized the payment of the transaction.

Because of the open nature of the system, it is conceivable that those who helped to authorize the transaction could be tracked down. Would they be prosecuted, though? Are they deemed partially responsible?

And, if a precedent is set and one group is prosecuted, what does that mean for the legal community going forward?

There is a Concern that Jobs Will be Lost

Implementing Blockchains means that companies will be able to get by with less staff and this could seem like a worrying thought at first when considering the world economy.

That said, who knows what kind of jobs may be created by that same technology? Take Bitcoin again, for example. In order to incentivize people to join the network and contribute the processing power of their computers, Bitcoins were offered.

Bitcoins can be used to pay for goods or sent to others. This lead to a movement of Bitcoin miners. Basically, people who were essentially paid for allowing the software to run on their computers.

Now, whilst this is not as profitable as it once was, it is actually a new industry and a whole new way to make money.

Should Blockchain be adopted on a larger scale, it is conceivable that a similar rewards system would need to be put in place and that more people would be able to earn money that way.

It would seem that the best option would be to adopt a wait and see policy on this one. New industry disruptors are emerging all the time and have made the more traditional industries more competitive instead of eclipsing them completely.

Look at Uber, for example. It has had a huge impact on traditional cabs and cab companies but has not replaced them completely. It has led to a whole new way for people to earn money and increase their dispos able income.

This, in itself, could lead to a stimulation of the economy rather than a contraction of it.

Considering the way in which technology is constantly changing the way that we live, it is not a stretch to think that the new disruptors that come about could boost job creation in ways we wouldn't have thought of yet.

Insufficient Numbers of Miners

Again, I am going to take Bitcoin as an example. Bitcoin miners earn coins by contributing computing power and authorizing transactions. They do have some incentive when it comes to maintaining the system because the value of the Bitcoins they own depends on this.

But what happens if the amount that the miners make is consistently outweighed by the costs that they incur for doing this?

They have to account for energy usage, opportunity cost, etc. And, whilst mining was quite easy early on, it now requires more specialized equipment that can be costly in itself.

You could join a pool of miners to increase computing power but that's no guarantee that you'll make any money.

Should the incentives prove inadequate to allow them to make a profit, how many new miners will be attracted by the idea? And, if there are no new miners, how will the network be able to sustain itself or even expand?

What happens if the miners decide overnight that the system isn't working for them? Or if a new player comes in with better incentives? What happens if the number of miners halves or quarters?

True, the data will not be lost. But will the system have the computing power to be able to continue running?

Big Business Could Hijack the System

Unfortunately, there is the distinct possibility that large corporates could hijack the system and make it work in their favor. It would be naïve to think that they would not try to do so.

It is conceivable, for example, that a company with deep enough pockets could pay someone to rewrite a portion of the blockchain.

If they offered the right incentives, it would be conceivable that they could convince enough people in the network to accept the changes.

History is not on our side with this one. Take the internet in general as an example. During the initial stages, it was argued that it could conceivably be used by large corporates to turn huge profits to the detriment of the users.

And it does seem that this fear was well-founded because that is exactly what has happened.

Will big business be able to hijack Blockchain technology and use it to make a huge profit? Will it remain a free and open-source commodity? That remains to be seen.

Complete Reliance on the System Could Be Dangerous

Whilst Blockchain systems are relatively safe and certainly a lot less vulnerable to being hacked than more traditional systems, it is conceivable that hackers could eventually find a way around this.

This possibility increases as the system becomes more widely used.

What happens if thieves are able to hack your Smart car, for example? They would be able to control the car remotely and do what they like with it.

There is No Central Control

This is both a positive and a negative. The lack of centralized control can help to keep the system honest, as it were.

The problem is that it has already become a stumbling block in the overall adoption of Blockchain systems and could cause problems in the future.

There are already so many different opinions on how to move Blockchain forward and squabbles within the ranks could lead to the Blockchain movement being halted completely.

No one seems to be able to agree on the best way to sustain Blockchain apps like Bitcoin. This lack of consensus here bodes badly for the future.

Decentralized control is a great idea in theory but it might not be as appealing when it comes to the actual practice.

Conclusion

We have just scratched the surface when it comes to Blockchain because it is so completely different to what we are accustomed to. One thing is for sure – it is going to forever change the way that we do many things going forward.

Blockchain could be as impactful as the development of the internet itself and the truth is that we cannot, even now, say exactly what the new applications of coding could entail.

Blockchain is possibly one of the most exciting developments when it comes to online security and as a catalyst for changing the way we view coding for ap

plications going forward.

What we do know is that it is going to have far-reach-

ing effects across a number of different industries.

Whilst it started as a way to secure the cryptocurren

cy, Bitcoin and whilst it is being looked on, at the

moment, as a major disruptor in the financial indus

try, its potential applications have much more far-

reaching consequences.

The future of the internet is well and truly here now,

and it is being built up block by block.

A message from the author, Steve Gold

To show my appreciation for your support, Id like to

offer you a free gifts:

FREE BONUS!

As a free bonus, I've included a preview of one

of my other best-selling books directly after

this section. Enjoy!

ALSO...

Be sure to check out my other books. Flip to the back of this book for a list of other books written by me.

Thank you again for your support.

Steve Gold

FREE BONUS!: Preview Of

"Elon Musk - The Biography of a

Modern Day Renaissance Man"!

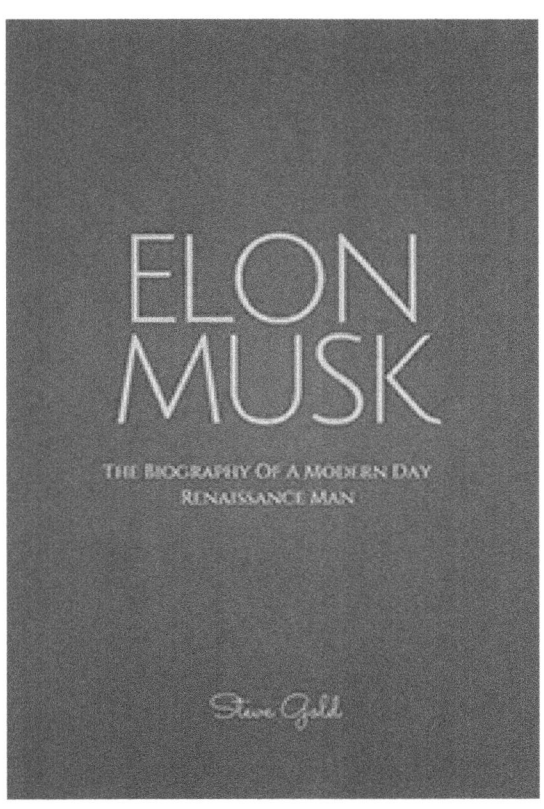

If you enjoyed this book, I have a little bonus for you; a preview of one of my other books "Elon Musk - The Biography of a Modern Day Renaissance Man". In this book, I take a closer look at exactly who Elon Musk is as well as examining the truly extraordinary accom plishments he has managed to achieve. Enjoy the free sample, and feel free to click on the purchase link be low if you would like to learn more about this truly incredible individual!

Introduction

When actor Robert Downey Jr. signed on to portray Tony Stark (a.k.a. Iron Man), he suggested to director John Favreau that they meet up with Elon Musk. They have a task of bringing to life a superhero, and Musk is the closest there ever is to Marvel's genius, billionaire, philanthropist in real life. The meeting was set and some of Musk's characteristics went into RDJ's portrayal of Tony Stark on screen, thus creating the memorable character that people come to know and love.

In reality, there is far more to Musk's life and person than can be personified by a fictional character. Sure, he does have a lot in common with Iron Man; he's a prodigious tech genius and entrepreneur, with the capacity to make seemingly impossible ideas a reality. Like Tony Stark, he dreams, thinks and lives large, but that is where the similarity ends.

Unlike his comic book counterpart, Elon Musk was not born into a life of luxury and ease. Despite showing potential for greatness as early as his preteens, his childhood and young adult life was filled with adversaries. To this day, Musk credits his early life struggles in helping him cultivate the indomitable spirit he is known for.

Having made his mark in the field of IT, finance, sustainable energy, automotive, aerospace manufacturing and space exploration, it is an understatement to say that Musk has come a long way from his humble beginnings. He founded some of the most pioneering companies – Paypal, Tesla Motors, and SpaceX – and is almost single-handed responsible for each enterprise's success. Whichever business he decided to dabble in, he brought with him a revolutionary idea which often ends up being a game-changer in the industry. Yet, he is far from done.

His brilliant mind never ceased to think up grander innovations, even after numerous repeated successful endeavors. His ample and wild ambitions, it seems, are driven by grand visions of changing the world we live in. His agenda for the future includes filling the roads with more electric cars, powering the world with solar energy, colonizing neighboring planets and en abling people to cover great distances with a futuristic high-speed public transportation system.

Most children would imagine of going outer space and travel to different cities in bullet-fast capsule pods, until those fantasies fade away in adulthood. Rarely are there individuals who dare to dream of living those fantasies that appropriately should stay within the realm of fiction. Elon Musk is among the excep tional few.

Chapter 1

The Beginnings Of Greatness

Almost every success story of high-achieving individuals contain episodes highlighting their extraordinary iron will, critical thinking, propensity for hard work, and an unwavering belief that the impossible is not out of their reach. As one of the most brilliant minds who help shaped the global economy after at the dawn of the information age and tech boom in the late 20th century, it is hardly surprising that Elon Musk displayed such distinctive personality traits at an incredibly young age.

Elon Reeve Musk was born in June 28 of 1971, in Pretoria, Gauteng, South Africa. His father is a South African-born British electrical engineer, Errol Musk, and his mother is Canadian-English dietitian, Maye Musk. Elon is the eldest of their three children, followed by brother Kimbal and sister Tosca.

Growing up in Pretoria, Elon's early years were far from a picture perfect childhood. His parents divorced when he was 9 years-old, after which he lived mostly with his demanding and emotionally abusive father. At school, he endured harsh bullying by his peers. In one notable instance, he ended up hospitalized after being pushed down a flight of stairs. Such ordeals led Elon to find solace in the safest company available; his own thoughts and imagination which resided in the deep recesses of his prodigious mind.

He would regularly immerse himself in reading as a means of escaping his troubles in the outside world. Encyclopedias and science fiction were among his favorite books; they added to his knowledge bank and encouraged his seemingly wild dreams of futuristic technology which had yet to become a reality. Often times, Elon would be caught daydreaming and lost in his own thoughts, ignoring the world around him in favor of the utopias in his imagination. Along with his innovative thoughts, Elon's childhood experiences also contributed to him developing a high tolerance for hardship and an extraordinary work ethic; attributes which he is well known for and which have served him well in his life.

His aptitude for technological innovations and entrepreneurship was evident when he began teaching himself computer programming at the tender age of 10. When he was just 12, he developed a spaceship shooter video game called, "Blastar", which he sold to a computer magazine for $500. After his first brush with success, Elon and his younger brother, Kimbal, hatched a plan to open an arcade near their school. Unfortunately, their enterprising plan had to be scrapped when their parents refused to provide the legal consent to obtain a business permit.

In 1988, after graduating from Pretoria Boys High School at the age of 17, Elon made the momentous decision to leave his hometown for the United States, without the support of his parents. This would be the first step towards his hard-earned success. He was able to obtain Canadian citizenship through his moth er a year later, and left South Africa for Montreal, Canada. There, he worked low-paying jobs and was living on the brink of poverty for a year.

At the age of 19, he was accepted into Queens University in Kingston, Ontario for undergraduate studies in science. It was during his studies that he met Canadi an author, Justine Musk, whom he would marry in 2000 and end up having six sons with. Their marriage lasted for only eight years, and Elon got married for the second time to British actress Talulah Riley. This marriage ended in divorce in 2014.

Two years into his studies at Queens, Elon received a scholarship from The University of Pennsylvania (Penn) in America. He relocated to the US in 1992, following his transfer to Penn. In the following year, he earned his Bachelor of Science degree in Physics from Penn's College of Arts and Sciences, and stayed back a year at Penn's Wharton School to complete his studies for a Bachelor of Science degree in Economics.

Throughout his college years, alongside his scientific studies, Elon took a keen interest in philosophical and religious literature. It was stated that his all-time favorite book is *The Hitchhiker's Guide to the Galaxy* by Douglas Adams. It is through this immersion in both science and personal studies of humanities that Elon found his calling; he had the lofty ambition of wanting to contribute to projects that would change the world for the better.

Consequently, his vision and entrepreneurial aspirations began taking shape, specifically in the areas of the internet, renewable energy and space exploration.

Check out the rest of "Elon Musk - The Biography of a Modern Day Renaissance Man" on Amazon.

Check Out My Other Books!

Elon Musk - The Biography Of A Modern Day Renaissance Man

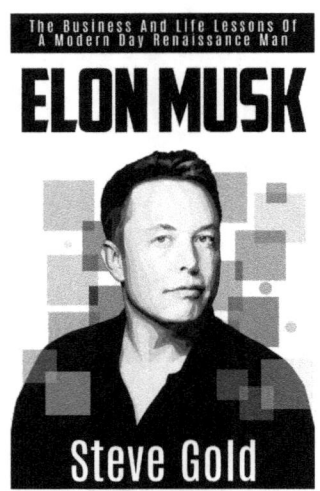

Elon Musk - The Business & Life Lessons Of A Modern Day Renaissance Man

Warren Buffett - The Business And Life Lessons Of An Investment Genius, Magnate And Philanthropist

Steve Jobs - The Biography & Lessons Of The Mastermind Behind Apple

Management - Achieve Management Excellence & World Class Leadership Skills In 7 Simple Steps

Sales - Easily Sell Anything To Anyone & Achieve Sales Excellence In 7 Simple Steps

Arduino - Getting Started With Arduino: The
Ultimate Beginner's Guide

All books available as ebooks or printed books